# THE WRITE THE BOOK HANDBOOK

HOW TO
WRITE, SELF-PUBLISH, MARKET AND SELL
YOUR OWN NON-FICTION BOOK

By
Frances Carryl

Thank you for purchasing The Write the Book Handbook: How to Write, Self-Publish, Market and Sell your own non-fiction book!

Copyright © 2023 Frances Carryl

All rights reserved. No part of this book may be reproduced or used in any manner without the prior written permission of the copyright owner, except for the use of brief quotations in a review.

To request permissions, contact the author at
writethebookgy@gmail.com

### DISCLAIMER

By reading this book, you acknowledge that I am not a licensed financial advisor, and that no Attorney-client relationship is hereby created. This book does not replace the advice of professionals. This book is in no way to be construed or substituted as financial, legal or other professional advice.

# Contents

Preface ................................................................................. 1

## Part 1: The Pre-writing Stage ............................... 16
The book's topic.................................................................17
The main idea ....................................................................18
The book's purpose...........................................................20
The book's genre...............................................................20
The audience .....................................................................22
The author..........................................................................24

## Part 2: The Writing Stage ..................................... 25
Outlining.............................................................................27
Drafting...............................................................................30
Revising ..............................................................................37
Editing.................................................................................40
Proofreading .....................................................................42

## Part 3: The Self-publishing Stage ......................... 43
Book Designing and Formatting ....................................44
Interior book design.........................................................45
Amazon Kindle Direct Publishing ..................................48
Proof and authors' copies ...............................................51

## Part 4: The Marketing and Selling Stage................... 53
Offline strategies ..............................................................53

To my sister, Tammy, and my parents,

Lavern Carryl and

the late, great Francis Augustus Carryl.

    Online strategies ............................................................... 54

    Taxes ..................................................................................... 56

Postface ....................................................................................... 57

The Author ................................................................................. 58

# Preface

It might interest you to know that about 81% of people want to write a book some-day.[1] However, only 3% actually do so, and only 20% of the ones who actually write the book, publish it![2] To say the least, these statistics are quite disheartening. Beyond the fact that they show just how few persons actually realize their dream of becoming authors, they also illustrate the magnitude of knowledge and experiences that were probably never shared because of the books that were never written.

Amongst the reasons given for not completing a book are the lack of know-how, perfection paralysis, procrastination, writer's block, and the perceived lack of time.[3] Although all of these are valid reasons, none of these should prevent anyone from accomplishing their book publishing dream, or sharing value with the world through print!

The goal of this book is to detail the exact steps you need to take to get your ideas on to shelves. In other words, this book takes care of the know-how aspect of completing your book.

---

[1] "81 Percent of People Want to Write a Book Someday …." *Meg Dowell Writes*, 9 Nov. 2017, https://megdowell.com/2017/11/09/81-percent-of-people-want-to-write-a-book-someday/ . Accessed 27 May. 2023.

[2] "The Top Reason People Never Finish Writing Their Book." *The Top Reason People Never Finish Writing Their Book – the Synergy Whisperer*, 20 Oct. 2015, https://thesynergyexpert.com/2015/10/20/the-top-reason-people-never-finish-writing-their-book/ Accessed 27 May. 2023.

[3] "The Top Reason People Never Finish Writing Their Book." *The Top Reason People Never Finish Writing Their Book – the Synergy Whisperer*, 20 Oct. 2015, https://thesynergyexpert.com/2015/10/20/the-top-reason-people-never-finish-writing-their-book/ Accessed 27 May. 2023.

The first part covers the pre-writing stage. Here is where we'll tackle all of the work that needs to be done before actual text production begins. You'll identify precisely what you want to write about, the purpose for writing your book, the audience you're writing to, who you are in relation to your book, the genre of your book, as well as other key preliminary considerations. In the second part of the book, we delve into thewriting process. Here is where we'll work towards communicating your thoughts and ideas in a cohesive and readable form. We'll consider outlining, drafting, editing andproofreading, and go from front cover to blurb and work through how each part of the book should be developed. By the third part of the book, you'll be ready to learn how to self-publishwhat you've written. At this stage, you'll be introduced to Amazon Kindle Direct Publishing (Amazon KDP) and learn how you can publish your work on Amazon, and have Amazon print and deliver those books directly to your customers directly, in exchange for a royalty payment. The fourth part of the book deals with marketing and selling your book. Here is where we'lldiscuss how you can draw and engage your target audience, as well as what you need to know about taxes.

Ultimately, by the end of this book, a considerable portion of yours should be done! Let's get started!

## Self-publishing FAQs

Before delving into the pre-writing process, let's consider a few questions which writers often ask early in the book-writing process.

- Should I write a book?
- How long should my book be?

- How long might this process take?
- How much does it cost to self-publish?
- What challenges am I likely to face?
- How much am I likely to earn?

These questions are critical because oftentimes persons form an interest in book-writing, and even commence the process, without knowing exactly what it takes to publish a book. This enthusiasm is in no way reproved. In fact, it is encouraged. It has often been said, "the things we have to learn before we can do them, we learn by doing them."[4] This is very true of the book-writing process.

Still, at some point, it becomes necessary to precisely determine what the book-writing process will require of you, and further, whether you're able to undertake it, at this time. Oftentimes, persons start the process only to later realize that the book they want to publish requires more time, money and information than they have at the time. Others later come to learn that the idea they earnestly want to share is more suitable for a blog, an article or even audio-visual communication. Alternatively, some realize that they truly have everything they need to start, and wonder why they hadn't started a long time ago.

For you to know how ready and equipped you are to undertake this journey, start by considering these six frequently asked

---

[4] A quote by Aristotle. "Learning by Doing Quotes (79 Quotes)." *Learning by Doing Quotes (79 Quotes)*, www.goodreads.com/quotes/tag/learning-by-doing#:~:text=%E2%80%9CFor%20the%20things%20we%20have,we%20learn%20by%20doing%20them.%E2%80%9D&text=%E2%80%9CIf%20somebody%20offers%20you%20an,how%20to%20do%20it%20later!%E2%80%9D&text=%E2%80%9CI%20have%20lost%20and%20loved,the%20person%20I%20am%20today.%E2%80%9D. Accessed 27 May. 2023.

questions. These will help you conceptualise what the road ahead looks like and make the appropriate decisions as early as possible.

## Should I write a book?

For some, writing a book on a topic they're passionate about is a no-brainer. It's the natural response to learning, experiencing and discovering what they have. For others, a bit more convincing is required, particularly in light of the time, money and effort it takes to get the job done. Regardless, of which category you fall into, it's important that you take the time to determine precisely why you want to publish your work since it's your reason(s) that will help keep you going when motivation and inspiration run thin along the way.

Perhaps writing may be your way of sharing valuable lessons with those who can benefit from your knowledge and experience. Or, you may be writing because publishing a book is one of your personal goals of yours. Another reason may be increasing your credibility in your sphere of work. Although publishing a book wouldn't make you an expert, it certainly suggests to others that you have an advanced appreciation of whatever you're writing about so much so that you're confident enough to put it into writing for others to see.

You may also be writing to expand your knowledge on a particular subject. Writing always requires extensive research and although you may not be an expert at the beginning of the process, by it's end, you can vastly increase your knowledge on your subject of choice.

Publishing your own book can also help build and expand your platform or business. If you're already known in a particular field or have a business that provides a particular service or product, publishing a book could increase your visibility and lead to increased clients, contacts and business. If you have neither a platform nor business, publishing a book is a great way to launch these.

It's also possible that you may be writing simply because you want to acquire clarity on a particular matter. Writing helps to streamline and clarify thoughts and ideas, and this could be an objective for writing your own book. Leslie Marmon Silko, a widely celebrated American author, said, *"I write in order to find out what I truly know and how I really feel about certain things. Writing requires me to go much deeper into my thoughts and memories than conversation does."*[5] For me, this was precisely the reason I wrote the book, *Grieving While Christian*. At the time, I was navigating through grief, and I wanted to understand exactly what I was feeling, and how I could reconcile a good God with my dad's death. To do this, I wrote, and the added benefit was sharing what I discovered with others.

What's your reason for writing a book? Discover it and keep it foremost on your mind as you continue along this journey.

---

[5] "Writers on Writing: Our Favorite Inspirational Quotes." *Writing Quotes by Writers That Inspire Us | Grammarly Blog*, 29 Sept. 2021, www.grammarly.com/blog/writing-quotes. Accessed 27 May. 2023.

## How long should my book be?

Broadly speaking, your book should be however long it needs to be to properly convey its message. To be more specific, the length of your book needs to accord with its genre.

Each book, depending on its genre, should attain a certain length in terms of words.[6] A book that is longer than average may appear too voluminous and time-consuming to get through,[7] while a book that is shorter than average may signal to readers that it is not sufficiently thorough or worthy of its price.[8]

Common genres in the non-fiction category include self-help books, historical books, academic texts, narrative journalism, travelogues, books on philosophy and insight, guides and 'how-to' manuals, personal essays and biographies, autobiographies and memoirs.[9] The closer your book is to the length expected in

---

[6] PhD, Beth Brombosz. "How Long Should a Nonfiction Book Be?" *Blogger to Author*, 16 June 2021, www.bloggertoauthor.com/how-long-should-my-nonfiction-book-be. Accessed 27 May. 2023.

[7] Portwood-Stacer, Laura. "How Long Should Your Academic Book and Book Chapters Be?." *Manuscript Works*, 13 Aug. 2019, https://manuscriptworks.com/blog/book-and-chapter-length Accessed 27 May. 2023.

[8] Dev-Dorrance. "Why Does Word Count Matter?" *Dorrance Publishing Company*, 23 Apr. 2020, https://www.dorrancepublishing.com/why-does-word-count-matter/. Accessed 27 May. 2023.

[9] "13 Types of Nonfiction (for You to Consider Writing)." *Self Publishing School*, 18 Oct. 2022, https://self-publishingschool.com/types-of-nonfiction/. Accessed 27 May. 2023.

these genres, the greater your chances of captivating readers who may not have heard of you before.[10]

Self-help books as well as guides and 'how-to' manuals can span around 40-000 to 50,000 words.[11] Still, it's typical to find shorter books in this category ranging from 20,000 to 25,000 words.[12] For, historical non-fiction books, these range between 70,000 words and 80,000 words.[13] On the higher end of the word-count scale are academic texts which range from 80,000 to 90,000 words,[14] and biographies, autobiographies and memoirs, which range from 80,000 to 200,000 words.[15] On the lower end are personal essays, narrative journalism pieces and travelogues with personal essays ranging from 800 to 15000

---

[10] Dev-Dorrance. "Why Does Word Count Matter?" *Dorrance Publishing Company*, 23 Apr. 2020, https://www.dorrancepublishing.com/why-does-word-count-matter/. Accessed 27 May. 2023.

[11] Lilly, Aida. "Ask Agent: Does Word Count Really Matter?" *Theword*, Theword, 28 June 2021, https://www.thewordfordiversity.org/post/ask-agent-does-word-count-really-matter. Accessed 27 May. 2023.

[12] Bloggertoauthor. "How Long Should a Nonfiction Book Be?" *Blogger to Author*, 15 July 2021, https://www.bloggertoauthor.com/how-long-should-my-nonfiction-book- Accessed 27 May. 2023.

[13] Lilly, Aida. "Ask Agent: Does Word Count Really Matter?" *Theword*, Theword, 28 June 2021, https://www.thewordfordiversity.org/post/ask-agent-does-word-count-really-matter. Accessed 27 May. 2023.

[14] Portwood-Stacer, Laura. "How Long Should Your Academic Book and Book Chapters Be?" *Manuscript Works*, Manuscript Works, 28 Dec. 2022, https://manuscriptworks.com/blog/book-and-chapter-length#:~:text=So%20here's%20a%20real%20answer,65%2C000%E2%80%9375%2C000%20words%20in%20length. Accessed 27 May. 2023.

[15] Lilly, Aida. "Ask Agent: Does Word Count Really Matter?" *Theword*, Theword, 28 June 2021, https://www.thewordfordiversity.org/post/ask-agent-does-word-count-really-matter. Accessed 27 May. 2023.

words,[16] narrative journalism pieces ranging from 3000 to 5000 words,[17] and travelogues ranging from 1500 to 1800 words.[18]

It is important that from the outset, you note the average length expected by your readers. With this in mind, you can set the appropriate word count for yourself, to ensure that you meet your readers' expectations.[19]

**How long might this process take?**

First time writers can take anywhere from 7 to 11 months to complete a book,[20] depending on how often they write, how much they write in one sitting, how much research is needed,

---

[16] Lockard, Trish. "Personal Essays Are Still a Hot Commodity." *Strikethewritetone*, Strikethewritetone, 1 Apr. 2022, https://www.strikethewritetone.com/post/personal-essays-are-still-a-hot-commodity#:~:text=A%20Good%20Length&text=Suggested%20word%20counts%20for%20the,average%20is%20800%E2%80%931%2C200%20words. Accessed 27 May. 2023.

[17] "Literary Journalism 2023." *Banff Centre*, https://www.banffcentre.ca/programs/literary-journalism/20230703#:~:text=Literary%20Journalism%20is%20designed%20for,(3%2C000%20%E2%80%93%205%2C000%20words). Accessed 27 May. 2023.

[18] "Long or Short Articles: Which Is Better for Travel Blogging?" *Travelpayouts Blog – Travel Partnership Platform*, 25 May 2022, https://www.travelpayouts.com/blog/length-of-the-articles/#:~:text=The%20perfect%20timeframe%20is%20no,%2C%20representing%201500%2D1800%20words. Accessed 27 May. 2023.

[19] Dev-Dorrance. "Why Does Word Count Matter?" *Dorrance Publishing Company*, 23 Apr. 2020, https://www.dorrancepublishing.com/why-does-word-count-matter/. Accessed 27 May. 2023.

[20] "How Long Does It Take to Write a Book & Do It Well?" *Self Publishing School*, 14 June 2022, https://self-publishingschool.com/how-long-does-it-take-to-write-a-book/. Accessed 27 May. 2023.

how much work is being outsourced, the waiting period while work is being outsourced, and a number of other factors that varies from author to author. Usually, the bulk of the time is dedicated to preparing the manuscript for publication, and publication itself, with the Amazon KDP tool, can take about 72 hours.[21]

## How much does it cost to self-publish?

The estimated cost of self-publishing a book ranges from about $150 to $2000.[22] This cost is largely dependent on the amount of work you complete by yourself as opposed to outsourcing. It is common for independent writers to outsource book cover design, copy-editing, proofreading, formatting for Amazon KDP and marketing. In fact, as far as is possible, unless skilled in these areas, writers should outsource these aspects of the process in order to guarantee the best results.

Home-made, amateur self-published books are very conspicuous to readers, and are known to look and read poorly. One way to avoid this and to ensure that your readers are not deterred from purchasing or finishing your book is to delegate aspects that you are not familiar with to professionals.

---

[21] *KDP Help Center Home - Amazon Kindle Direct Publishing.* https://kdp.amazon.com/en_US/help. Accessed 27 May. 2023.

[22] McCrary-Ruiz-Esparza, Emily, and Elizabeth Mikotowicz says: "How Much Does It Cost to Self Publish a Book." *Written Word Media*, 5 July 2022, https://www.writtenwordmedia.com/cost-to-self-publish/#:~:text=The%20estimated%20total%20cost%20to,others%20spend%20nothing%20at%20all. Accessed 27 May. 2023.

Fiverr is an online marketplace where you can find persons to affordably design your book cover as well as edit, proofread, format and promote your book.[23] According to your budget, you can choose the range that you're willing to pay, and review the profile of sellers to ascertain their experience with the service that you're seeking.

**What challenges am I likely to face?**

The *Write the Book Handbook* provides you with the necessary know-how to make your book a reality. However, know-how is not the only resource required. Writing, self-publishing, selling and marketing a book also takes time and effort, and these resources, in particular, cannot be purchased, taught or outsourced. Therefore, finding the time and making the effort can prove challenging at times. However, the only way to overcome these challenges is to decidedly and intentionally make the time to write, and to write even when it's hard to do so. "In fact, many professional writers insist on writing No. Matter. What".[24]

Another common challenge is writers' block or the "feeling of being stuck in the writing process without the ability to move

---

[23] Fiverr - *Freelance Services Marketplace for Businesses*. www.fiverr.com/support/articles/360010558038. Accessed 27 May. 2023.

[24] Joki, Kimberly. "4 Ways to Find Writing Inspiration and Finish Your Work." *Writing Inspiration to Stop Writer's Block | Grammarly*, Grammarly Blog, 7 June 2017, https://www.grammarly.com/blog/writing-inspiration-ideas/?gclid=Cj0KCQiAtbqdBhDvARIsAGYnXBNoWllUfz68aHZ0A-.

forward and write anything new".[25] It's mainly triggered by stress, interpersonal frustration, apathy, and disappointment.[26] Needless to say, this can be quite daunting and frustrating, and what's ironic is that the best way to overcome it is by writing.[27] For Maya Angelou, she says,

> What I try to do is write. I may write for two weeks 'the cat sat on the mat, that is that, not a rat.' And it might be just the most boring and awful stuff. But I try. When I'm writing, I write. And then it's as if the muse is convinced that I'm serious and says, 'Okay. Okay. I'll come.[28]

---

[25] https://www.masterclass.com/articles/what-is-writers-block-how-to-overcome-writers-block-with-step-by-step-guide-and-writing-exercises Accessed 27 May. 2023.

[26] Joki, Kimberly. "4 Ways to Find Writing Inspiration and Finish Your Work." *Writing Inspiration to Stop Writer's Block | Grammarly*, 27 May 2019, www.grammarly.com/blog/writing-inspiration-ideas/?gclid=Cj0KCQiAtbqdBhDvARIsAGYnXBNoWllUfz68aHZ0A-fUpjgaDV7X7HItwJ2A3M0XKqJWVsZJa7AVKDcaAmHREALw_wcB&gclsrc=aw.ds. Accessed 27 May. 2023.

[27] Joki, Kimberly. "4 Ways to Find Writing Inspiration and Finish Your Work." *Writing Inspiration to Stop Writer's Block | Grammarly*, 27 May 2019, www.grammarly.com/blog/writing-inspiration-ideas/?gclid=Cj0KCQiAtbqdBhDvARIsAGYnXBNoWllUfz68aHZ0A-fUpjgaDV7X7HItwJ2A3M0XKqJWVsZJa7AVKDcaAmHREALw_wcB&gclsrc=aw.ds. Accessed 27 May. 2023.

[28] Joki, Kimberly. "4 Ways to Find Writing Inspiration and Finish Your Work." *Writing Inspiration to Stop Writer's Block | Grammarly*, 27 May 2019, www.grammarly.com/blog/writing-inspiration-ideas/?gclid=Cj0KCQiAtbqdBhDvARIsAGYnXBNoWllUfz68aHZ0A-fUpjgaDV7X7HItwJ2A3M0XKqJWVsZJa7AVKDcaAmHREALw_wcB&gclsrc=aw.ds. Accessed 27 May. 2023.

Many writers also suffer from perfection paralysis. This is the immobilizing fear of failure.[29] It causes immense stress and results in writers either procrastinating or ceasing the writing process altogether. Akin to imposter syndrome, it can result from the feeling of not being good enough to write on the chosen subject.[30] To overcome this, it's best to recall that perfection is a farce that no-one has attained, including your readers.[31] Your best is good enough and done is better than perfect. You also need to disrupt the "all or nothing approach" and break down tasks into smaller more manageable pieces.[32] This would lead to more frequent feelings of accomplishment and reassure you that you're capable to completing your book.[33]

---

[29] *Forbes*, www.forbes.com/sites/reganwalsh/2018/10/08/3-steps-to-overcoming-perfection-paralysis/?sh=30186aff5901. Accessed 27 May. 2023.

[30] "Perfection Paralysis and How To Overcome It | So How's Therapy Podcast." *Cohesive Therapy NYC*, 24 Mar. 2022, https://cohesivetherapynyc.com/blog/perfection-paralysis-with-karen-conlon-lcsw/ Accessed 27 May. 2023.

[31] Drillinger, Meagan. "7 Steps to Breaking the 'Perfectionism, Procrastination, Paralysis' Cycle." *Healthline*, www.healthline.com/health/anxiety/7-steps-to-breaking-the-perfectionism-procrastination-paralysis-cycle#2.-Keep-your-tasks-bite-sized. Accessed 27 May. 2023.

[32] Drillinger, Meagan. "7 Steps to Breaking the 'Perfectionism, Procrastination, Paralysis' Cycle." *Healthline*, www.healthline.com/health/anxiety/7-steps-to-breaking-the-perfectionism-procrastination-paralysis-cycle#2.-Keep-your-tasks-bite-sized. Accessed 27 May. 2023.

[33] Drillinger, Meagan. "7 Steps to Breaking the 'Perfectionism, Procrastination, Paralysis' Cycle." *Healthline*, www.healthline.com/health/anxiety/7-steps-to-breaking-the-perfectionism-

What's clear is that challenges will arise throughout the journey. Writing a book, though immensely simplified with the advent of technology, is not the easiest thing to do. It will cost you, and this should be neither alarming nor deterring. Simply remember your reason for writing and take things one sentence at a time.

## How much am I likely to earn?

If you're writing a book solely to earn money, it may be wiser to invest in another venture. Books are unpredictable sources of income. The amount of money you make depends on the price of the book, the percentage of your royalty payment, and how many books you sell.

The price of the book would vary based on the book's genre and format. For instance, the average cost of an academic text ranges between $80 and $150,[34] whereas the average price of a self-help book is between $10 and $20.[35] As it relates to format, digital books (ebooks) tend to be much cheaper than paperbacks, and paperbacks are often cheaper than hardcover

---

procrastination-paralysis-cycle#2.-Keep-your-tasks-bite-sized. Accessed 27 May. 2023.

[34] Melanie Hanson, Average Cost of College Textbooks, *Education Data Initiative*, https://educationdata.org/average-cost-of-college-textbooks#:~:text=Hard%20copy%20books%20can%20cost,12%25%20with%20each%20new%20edition. Accessed 27 May. 2023.

[35] "How to Price Your Self-Published Book: Everything You Need to Know -." *The Self Publisher*, 8 Dec. 2020, https://theselfpublisher.com/how-to-price-your-self-published-book/ Accessed 27 May. 2023.

books.[36] Of course, the length of the book is also a consideration with longer books attracting a higher cost.

When setting your price, it's best to ensure that the price is in accordance with what's usual for books in that genre and format. If your book is underpriced, readers may assume that the book is of a low quality, and if it's over-priced, they may question whether the book is actually worth its cost.[37] A brief search in bookstores and online marketplaces should help you ascertain what's reasonable in your circumstances.

In terms of royalty payments, you should also note that Amazon KDP offers a fixed royalty rate of 60% on paperbacks. For ebooks, the royalty rate is either 35% or 70%.[38] In any event, these percentages may change from time to time. It's therefore best to check the Amazon website for updates on the percentages and calculations.

In terms of your expected amount of sales, consider that on average, for non-fiction books, self-help books, academic texts, books on history, travelogues and biographies, autobiographies

---

[36] How to Price Your Self-Published Book: Everything You Need to Know -." *The Self Publisher*, 8 Dec. 2020, https://theselfpublisher.com/how-to-price-your-self-published-book/ Accessed 27 May. 2023.

[37] How to Price Your Self-Published Book: Everything You Need to Know -." *The Self Publisher*, 8 Dec. 2020, https://theselfpublisher.com/how-to-price-your-self-published-book/ Accessed 27 May. 2023.

[38] "Digital Book Pricing Page." *Digital Book Pricing Page*, https://kdp.amazon.com/en_US/help/topic/G200634500 Accessed 27 May. 2023.

and memoirs are amongst the most popular on Amazon.[39] Still, it is common for a self-published book to sell around 250 copies within its lifetime.[40] It could be more or less depending on the book's topic, its quality, demand from readers, marketing efforts, and other like variables.[41] Regardless, as long as you promote your book and leave it posted on Amazon, you should be able to earn an income from it for as long as you want to.

---

[39] "What Are the Most Popular Book Genres on Amazon?" *Self Publishing School*, 18 Nov. 2021, https://self-publishingschool.com/most-popular-book-genres-on-amazon/ Accessed 27 May. 2023.

[40] "How to Self-Publish a Book and Sell Over 250 Copies – Tagari.com." *How to Self-Publish a Book and Sell Over 250 Copies – Tagari.com*, 17 Feb. 2022, https://www.tagari.com/how-many-copies-does-the-average-self-published-book-sell/ Accessed 27 May. 2023.

[41] "How to Self-Publish a Book and Sell Over 250 Copies – Tagari.com." *How to Self-Publish a Book and Sell Over 250 Copies – Tagari.com*, 17 Feb. 2022, https://www.tagari.com/how-many-copies-does-the-average-self-published-book-sell/ Accessed 27 May. 2023

# Part 1

# The Pre-writing Stage

> "Writing is really a way of thinking—not just feeling but thinking about things that are disparate, unresolved, mysterious, problematic, or just sweet."[42]

Pre-writing is the process of generating and clarifying ideas before you begin writing.[43] It is familiarly called the "talking stage" of writing.[44] It's where you "talk" about "what", "how", "why" and "to whom" you want to write in order to better convey your ideas when writing.[45]

One of the pre-writing techniques is "asking questions".[46] By asking and answering pointed questions, you're better able to

---

[42] "How to Prewrite: Prewriting Tips for Generating Ideas." *How to Prewrite: Prewriting Tips for Generating Ideas | Grammarly*, 28 June 2022, www.grammarly.com/blog/prewrite. Accessed 27 May. 2023.

[43] "Prewriting Strategies." *Prewriting Strategies | KU Writing Center*, https://writing.ku.edu/prewriting-strategie Accessed 27 May. 2023.

[44] "Prewriting Stage of the Writing Process Includes Talk." *ThoughtCo*, 1 July 2019, www.thoughtco.com/prewriting-stage-of-the-writing-process-8492. Accessed 27 May. 2023.

[45] "Prewriting Stage of the Writing Process Includes Talk." *ThoughtCo*, 1 July 2019, www.thoughtco.com/prewriting-stage-of-the-writing-process-8492. Accessed 27 May. 2023.

[46] "Prewriting Stage of the Writing Process Includes Talk." *ThoughtCo*, 1 July 2019, www.thoughtco.com/prewriting-stage-of-the-writing-process-8492. Accessed 27 May. 2023.

appreciate where you are with your work and where you want to be. Let's consider the following six questions.

- What topic will I be writing on?
- What is the book's main idea?
- What is the book's purpose?
- What is the book's genre?
- Who is my target audience?
- Who am I in relation to this book?

Although answering these questions is not part and parcel of actual text production, its importance should not be overlooked. When we complete this stage, we're better able to cohesively develop our ideas one concept at a time and reduce the likelihood of feeling stuck along away.[47] Beyond this, some of the work done at this stage can make its way into the final text of the book, or the materials used to market it. For instance, when we identify and clearly articulate the purpose of our book, we can use the same expression in the preface or blurb of our book. Also, when we establish who we are in relation to the book, we can utilise the same terminology when preparing a personal statement for marketing purposes.

## The book's topic

It's no surprise that you need to decide what topic, subject, or issue you want to write about. It may be relationships, children, business, religion, cars, food or otherwise. Whatever it is, this is

---

[47] "How to Prewrite: Prewriting Tips for Generating Ideas." *How to Prewrite: Prewriting Tips for Generating Ideas | Grammarly*, 28 June 2022, www.grammarly.com/blog/prewrite. Accessed 27 May. 2023.

your starting point and this decision will determine both the direction and content of your book.

Beyond identifying the topic, it's important that you ensure that it is relevant, not overly discussed, and still not so obscure that no-one might be interested in it. At all times, we must be reminded that we are not writing the book to ourselves. The book is being written for an audience, and as such, it is important to consider whether other persons would be interested in your topic, and whether there is scope for a fresh and new perspective on the subject.

One way of discovering whether your topic is relevant, sought after, and yet still unique enough to write about, is by searching bookstores both online and offline. If there are many books on the same subject, this is a good indicator that persons are interested in your chosen topic. Also, if you're able to identify a gap or missing perspective, this means that there's an opportunity for you to share your unique perspective on the subject.

## The main idea

After identifying your topic, the next pivotal question you need to ask is, "what do I want my readers to know about this topic"? The answer to this question constitutes the main idea of your book.[48]

---

[48] "Finding the main idea" https://www.mpc.edu/home/showdocument?id=12790#:~:text=What%20is%20a%20main%20idea,idea%20in%20a%20single%20sentence. Accessed 27 May. 2023.

Even if you've begun writing or already have some amount of content for your book, it's important that you pause and take the time to clarify precisely what central point you wish to make to your readers.[49] Without a clear concept of this, you run the risk of writing an incoherent piece of work with no clearly communicated message.[50] You're also more likely to become stuck and unsure of what thoughts you ought to be developing along the way. You might also find it somewhat difficult to effectively articulate the gist of your book when someone else asks what it is about.

For many, writers ought to be able to effortlessly express what their book is about in no more than three sentences or 10 seconds.[51] Intentionally developing your main idea is a sure way of quickly explaining to potential readers what they can expect from your book.

Identifying the main idea also helps you to ascertain how knowledgeable you are on what you want to write about. A book requires much more information than what is needed for an essay, a speech or a presentation. As such, it often requires extensive research no matter how experienced or well

---

[49] "Finding the main idea" https://www.mpc.edu/home/showdocument?id=12790#:~:text=What%20is%20a%20main%20idea,idea%20in%20a%20single%20sentence. Accessed 27 May. 2023.

[50] "Finding the main idea" https://www.mpc.edu/home/showdocument?id=12790#:~:text=What%20is%20a%20main%20idea,idea%20in%20a%20single%20sentence. Accessed 27 May. 2023.

[51] jerichowriters. "How to Write an Elevator Pitch for Your Novel (With Examples) | Jericho Writers." *Jericho Writers*, 10 Nov. 2020, https://jerichowriters.com/how-to-write-an-elevator-pitch-for-your-novel/ Accessed 27 May. 2023.

informed you may be on the subject. By plainly outlining your main idea, you can form a clear sense of what you need to research and how much more information you might need to gather.

## The book's purpose

After you've conceptualised what your book will be about, you need to clarify what you want it to accomplish in your readers.[52] Every book ought to leave its readers with value, and every writer needs to know precisely what value their book will add to their readers.[53] In this way, you're better able to filter through the irrelevant ideas that may pop-up and stick to those ideas that are supportive of the book's objective.

## The book's genre

A book's genre is essentially its literary category.[54] Common genres for non-fiction books include self-help books, historical

---

[52] Lawrence, Arlyn. "Developing Your Book's Purpose Statement &Mdash; Inspira Literary Solutions." *Inspira Literary Solutions*, 18 Nov. 2018, www.inspiralit.com/blog/2018/11/18/developing-your-books-purpose-statement. Accessed 27 May. 2023.

[53] Lawrence, Arlyn. "Developing Your Book's Purpose Statement &Mdash; Inspira Literary Solutions." *Inspira Literary Solutions*, 18 Nov. 2018, www.inspiralit.com/blog/2018/11/18/developing-your-books-purpose-statement. Accessed 27 May. 2023.

[54] Chase, Joslyn. "Book Genre: Why Figuring Out Your Genre Will Help Your Story Succeed." *The Write Practice*, 7 Dec. 2020, https://thewritepractice.com/book-genre-story-success/#:~:text=Book%20genre%20provides%20a%20directory,genre%20shelf%20is%20so%20important. Accessed 27 May. 2023.

books, academic texts, 'how-to' manuals, personal essays and biographies, autobiographies and memoirs.[55]

It is critical that you ascertain precisely which genre your book will fall into since this will ultimately determine your readers' expectations in terms of length, tone, style, structure and content.[56] It also determines where your book will be placed on the shelves of book-stores, or categorized on the Amazon KDP interface.[57] For instance, the tone of a 'how-to' manual is not as formal as an academic text. Neither is it likely to be as long or formally structured. It may also be displayed in a different part of a book-store and marketed to a different audience on Amazon. As such, it is wise to ascertain the genre within which your book is best placed, and aim to meet the expectations of readers associated with that category.

Of course, when writing, the lines between genres may become blurred. For instance, aspects of a self-help book may become academic when discussing serious topics, and there may be similarities in the way in which historical books and academic texts are written. Still, it is extremely important that you

---

[55] "13 Types of Nonfiction (for You to Consider Writing)." *Self Publishing School*, 9 May 2022, https://self-publishingschool.com/types-of-nonfiction/ Accessed 27 May. 2023.

[56] Bransford, Nathan. "Why It's Important to Know Your Book's Genre." *Nathan Bransford | Writing, Book Editing, Publishing*, 11 Apr. 2018, https://nathanbransford.com/blog/2018/04/why-its-important-to-know-your-genre Accessed 27 May. 2023.

[57] Chase, Joslyn. "Book Genre: Why Figuring Out Your Genre Will Help Your Story Succeed." *The Write Practice*, 7 Dec. 2020, https://thewritepractice.com/book-genre-story-success/#:~:text=Book%20genre%20provides%20a%20directory,genre%20shelf%20is%20so%20important. Accessed 27 May. 2023.

identify the single genre with which your book will mostly align, and stick to it.⁵⁸

## The audience

It's tempting to aim to write a book that everyone will want to read. However, such an attempt is neither plausible nor likely to be successful simply because in seeking to reach everyone, the book may reach no-one.

Consider what would happen if you placed multiple buckets into a bathroom and turned on the shower. It's likely that some of the buckets may never capture any water, and for those that do, the amount of water they capture in a short time would likely be minimal. Instead, it's far more effective to take a targeted approach, select a bucket and turn on a pipe directly above it. In the same way, writers have a better chance of effectively conveying their message when they direct it towards a specific group.

Defining an audience helps you to brainstorm your content, identify the needs to be addressed, focus your message, decide your tone, focus your marketing efforts and ultimately secure the best possible sales.⁵⁹ In addition to this, it also helps you to remain conscious of the fact that you are not writing to yourself.

---

[58] Bransford, Nathan. "Why It's Important to Know Your Book's Genre." *Nathan Bransford | Writing, Book Editing, Publishing*, 11 Apr. 2018, https://nathanbransford.com/blog/2018/04/why-its-important-to-know-your-genre Accessed 27 May. 2023.

[59] "How to Identify Your Book's Audience." https://greenleafbookgroup.com/learning-center/book-creation/how-to-identify-your-books-

Although it's seemingly self-evident that the book you're writing is for someone else, because writing requires you to be vulnerable and to rely on your personal experiences, it becomes easy to forget that you're not writing to yourself. As such, when we intentionally decide precisely whom the book is being written to, we can be more readily reminded that the book has its own audience.

One way in which you can define your audience is by creating a readers' profile. This can be done by asking pointed questions such as:

- what is my readers' age-range;
- is my reader married;
- what is the educational level of my reader;
- what is my reader's religion;
- where does my reader live;
- what is my reader's job;
- how familiar is my reader with this topic;
- what does my reader need; and so forth.

Of course, the type of questions you ask will depend on the topic of your book. For instance, the marital status of your reader is likely irrelevant if you're writing a children's book, and the address of your reader is likely irrelevant if you're writing a faith-based book. Still, the idea is to specifically define

---

audience#:~:text=One%20of%20the%20important%20components,once%20your%20book%20is%20published. Accessed 27 May. 2023.

the relevant needs and characteristics of your readers and keep them in mind throughout the writing process.

## The author

You need to know what qualifies you to write your book. This isn't necessarily restricted to professional or vocational qualifications. In fact, depending on your book's topic, your professional and vocational qualifications may not be relevant, at all. What may be more relevant is your experience, a skill, a place you have lived, a country you visited, a job you once had, or even a disability you're living with. Whatever it is, you need to know why you're a suitable candidate for writing your book.

Knowing who you are in relation to your book ensures your ability to convince readers that you're a credible source of information on your chosen topic. This is extremely critical when marketing your book since as a self-published author, you're the one that has to gain the trust of your potential readers and convince them to buy from you. This means that in some sense, you're essentially selling yourself. To do this effectively, you need to pause and develop a personal statement or short biography about yourself including the accolades, skills and experience relevant to your topic. It's also useful to point your readers to any social media platforms through which they can learn more, and interact with you.

Notably, the information shared in your short biography can also be used when writing the preface, blurb, or the "About the Author" section of your book. You can also use the same or similar expressions when preparing marketing materials such as social media posts, newsletters, newspaper briefs about your book and answers to interview questions.

# Part 2

# The Writing Stage

"Work on a good piece of writing proceeds on three levels: a musical one, where it is composed; an architectural one, where it is constructed; and finally, a textile one, where it is woven.[60]"

The writing stage is the point where you translate your thoughts and ideas into a clear and easily readable form.[61] This process usually entails outlining, drafting, revising, editing and proofreading.[62] For some, the idea of a step-by-step process may seem dull and constraining. It is perhaps more enticing to view writing as a totally organic and unrestricted task that culminates in a perfect piece of work. However, this is an unrealistic expectation for most if not everyone.

---

[60] "Writing Process Quotes (1360 Quotes)." *Writing Process Quotes (1360 Quotes)*, https://www.goodreads.com/quotes/tag/writing-process Accessed 27 May. 2023.

[61] "Overview of the Writing Process; Hunter College." https://www.hunter.cuny.edu/rwc/handouts/the-writing-process-1/invention/Overview-of-the-Writing-Process Accessed 27 May. 2023.

[62] "The Writing Process: 6 Steps Every Writer Should Know." *The Writing Process: 6 Steps Every Writer Should Know | Grammarly*, 12 May 2021, https://www.grammarly.com/blog/writing-process/?gclid=CjwKCAiAh9qdBhAOEiwAvxIok0ogSvNq5t50-S-Z6JiLodgto7TMcwlXfNOtXSeLDFYKRTY15iSm0xoChy0QAvD_BwE&gclsrc=aw.ds Accessed 27 May. 2023.

Even seasoned writers adhere to some version of a step-by-step writing process.[63] More than ensuring that the task is broken down into manageable and attainable steps, the step-by-step writing process helps writers to avert stress, anxiety and the feeling of being stuck.[64] Further, with smaller tasks, writers are able to focus on specific aspects of the book in order to produce a better quality of work.[65]

Of course, stages will overlap.[66] Many begin drafting while outlining and many revise and edit while drafting. Writing is a fluid process, and so moving back and forth is expected.[67] Even so, as a young writer, you are encouraged to use the step-by-

---

[63] Joanne Kathleen Rowling, the author of the Harry Potter series, is one such author. McNulty, Bridget, and View Archive; "Writing Tips From J.K. Rowling | Now Novel." *Now Novel*, 8 Oct. 2012 https://www.nownovel.com/blog/five-great-writing-tips-from-j-k-rowling/ Accessed 27 May. 2023.

[64] Athuraliya, Amanda, and View all posts by Amanda Athuraliya; "The Essential 5-Step Writing Process for All Writers." *Creately Blog*, 10 Mar. 2020, https://creately.com/blog/marketing-sales/writing-process-steps/ Accessed 27 May. 2023.

[65] Athuraliya, Amanda, and View all posts by Amanda Athuraliya; "The Essential 5-Step Writing Process for All Writers." *Creately Blog*, 10 Mar. 2020, https://creately.com/blog/marketing-sales/writing-process-steps/ Accessed 27 May. 2023.

[66] "Overview of the Writing Process; Hunter College." https://www.hunter.cuny.edu/rwc/handouts/the-writing-process-1/invention/Overview-of-the-Writing-Process Accessed 27 May. 2023.

[67] "PROCESS WRITING." *PROCESS WRITING*, http://www.buowl.boun.edu.tr/teachers/PROCESS%20WRITING.htm#:~:text=Writing%20is%20a%20fluid%20process,writing%20process%20in%20their%20writing. Accessed 27 May. 2023.

step process because of the structure and clarity that it will add to your writing experience.[68]

## Outlining

Outlining is the process of determining your book's potential structure.[69] It's where you develop the skeleton or roadmap for your book.[70] This helps you visualize your main points, decide how they are connected, and organize how they will flow and support the main idea of your book.[71] Simply put, your book outline lets you know exactly where you're going. This helps you write more quickly and avoid the dreaded writer's block.[72]

To start, you need to decide how you intend to structure your book. That is, whether you'll be using a "step-by-step" structure,

---

[68] "PROCESS WRITING." *PROCESS WRITING*, http://www.buowl.boun.edu.tr/teachers/PROCESS%20WRITING.htm#:~:text=Writing%20is%20a%20fluid%20process,writing%20process%20in%20their%20writing. Accessed 27 May. 2023.

[69] "Outlining." *The Writing Center*, https://writingcenter.gmu.edu/writing-resources/writing-as-process/outlining Accessed 27 May. 2023.

[70] "The Writing Process: 6 Steps Every Writer Should Know." *The Writing Process: 6 Steps Every Writer Should Know | Grammarly*, 12 May 2021, https://www.grammarly.com/blog/writing-process/?gclid=CjwKCAiAh9qdBhAOEiwAvxIok-24X4osuk2INZS8PkWBZg73X2_-BbFChG-I9m2Fg16uMKnK9V8nahoCswcQAvD_BwE&gclsrc=aw.ds Accessed 27 May. 2023.

[71] "Outlining." *The Writing Center*, https://writingcenter.gmu.edu/writing-resources/writing-as-process/outlining Accessed 27 May. 2023.

[72] "Book Outline: How to Outline a Book [Template Included]." *SelfPublishing.com : The #1 Resource for Self-Publishing a Book* https://selfpublishing.com/book-outline/ Accessed 27 May. 2023.

a chronological structure, or an essay structure.[73] The structure of your book is important because it helps your readers to easily comprehend and connect with the message being shared.[74]

The "step-by-step" structure is best suited for guides and 'how-to' manuals. The essence of this structure is a clear, logical and actionable sequence that conveys the main idea to the reader.[75] On the other hand, the chronological structure sets out a series of events in the order that they occurred. As such, this structure is suitable for biographies, autobiographies and memoirs.[76] With respect to the essay structure, this is appropriate for any book whose main idea can be developed in the same way that an essay can.[77] That is, with an introduction that presents an idea, a body that develops the idea, and a conclusion that summarizes what the book was about.

With your book's structure in mind, you can proceed to outline your book. One effective way of doing this is by utilizing the "chapter-by-chapter" method. This is where you note all of the

---

[73] https://blog.reedsy.com/guide/nonfiction/how-to-outline-a-nonfiction-book/

[74] "Non-Fiction Text Features and Text Structure." *This Reading Mama*, https://thisreadingmama.com/comprehension/non-fiction/non-fiction-text-structure/ Accessed 27 May. 2023.

[75] "Outlining a Nonfiction Book: 3 Steps to Success." *Reedsy*, https://blog.reedsy.com/guide/nonfiction/how-to-outline-a-nonfiction-book/ Accessed 27 May. 2023.

[76] "Outlining a Nonfiction Book: 3 Steps to Success." *Reedsy*, https://blog.reedsy.com/guide/nonfiction/how-to-outline-a-nonfiction-book/ Accessed 27 May. 2023.

[77] "Outlining a Nonfiction Book: 3 Steps to Success." *Reedsy*, https://blog.reedsy.com/guide/nonfiction/how-to-outline-a-nonfiction-book/ Accessed 27 May. 2023.

key points, ideas or principles you want to put forward and group them into chapters. In other words, this is where you create the "Table of Contents" for your book, and go on to briefly explain what each chapter will be about.

Your chapter titles don't need to be perfect at this point. What is more important is knowing what each chapter will be about. For this purpose, a chapter overview of about one or two sentences should be sufficient. The goal is to make sure that you're clear on what your ideas are, and how they will be developed. You also need to ensure that the content in your potential chapters will not be repetitive or redundant.

Below is a working outline for a non-fiction book with an essay structure.

- Cover
- Dedication
- Copyright and Disclaimer
- Preface
- Chapters
- Postface
- About the Author
- Blurb

You can flesh out your outline in the "Write the Book Activity Sheets" available at https://writethebookgy.com/ . Once that is complete, you couldconsider most of your work done. Some say, the outline itself is 95% of the work.[78] However, you should note that your book outline will likely change along the way.

---

[78] According to international bestselling author, Jeffrey Deaver, the outline is 95 percent of the book and writing is the easy part. "Book Outline: How to Outline a Book [Template Included]." *SelfPublishing.com : The #1*

In fact, "[a] good book outline changes and develops as you write".[79] Chapter titles, chapter content, the number of chapters, and so forth, can change during the process. In some sense, as you write, the book itself will decide the way it should be developed. This is completely normal, expected, and should be embraced.

## Drafting

In the words of American novelist, editor and professor, E. L. Doctorow,

> [p]lanning to write is not writing. Outlining, researching, talking to people about what you're doing, none of that is writing. Writing is writing.

This is the point where you begin to put your ideas into sentences and paragraphs. Whether you choose to write or to type, now is the time to use the outline you created and build your first draft, line upon line. It doesn't need to be perfect, and it doesn't need to be done in a day, a week, or a month. It just needs to reflect what's been in your head and your heart up until this point.

To get you started, here are a few pointers on drafting the various parts of your book.

---

*Resource for Self-Publishing a Book*, https://selfpublishing.com/book-outline/ Accessed 27 May. 2023.

[79] According to international bestselling author, Jeffrey Deaver, the outline is 95 percent of the book and writing is the easy part. "Book Outline: How to Outline a Book [Template Included]." *SelfPublishing.com : The #1 Resource for Self-Publishing a Book*, https://selfpublishing.com/book-outline/ Accessed 27 May. 2023.

- Title- In simple terms, your book's title should be "M.A.D". That is, memorable, attention-grabbing and capable of delivering the book's overall message.[80] This is because the title is the first thing your readers will likely interact with. This is what lets them know what they can expect, whether your book will meet their needs and overall, whether your book is worthy of their purchase.

- Dedication- This is a completely optional section where you mention, give thanks or acknowledge a person or group of persons whom you wish to honour. To write this section you simply need to identify who you want to honour and say exactly what you want to say to or about them. One great way to get started on this is by reading a few dedication pages for ideas on how you might want to phrase your own.

- Copyright and Disclaimer- A copyright notice is important because it declares to your readers that you own the copyright to your work.[81] It is often accompanied by a statement that says that you reserve all the formal rights that copyright protection grants you such as

---

[80] Christian McClean, "How To Write a Nonfiction Book that Sells: A Comprehensive Guide" *CEM Writing Services*, https://www.cemwritingservices.com/blog/2020/12/20/the-ultimate-nonfiction-book-guide Accessed 27 May. 2023.

[81] "Outlining a Nonfiction Book: 3 Steps to Success." *Reedsy*, https://blog.reedsy.com/guide/nonfiction/how-to-outline-a-nonfiction-book/ Accessed 27 May. 2023.

reproduction and distribution.[82] On the other hand, a disclaimer is an official statement that seeks to release you from any legal responsibility for the contents of your book.[83] The exact terminology used to declare your copyright, reserve your rights or release you from liability should be based on the advice of a legal practitioner.

- Preface- A preface is a short introductory essay providing the context for your book.[84] It usually includes the source of your book's inspiration, why you are qualified to write on your topic, and what your readers can expect to gain by reading your book.[85] It should be brief, engaging and informative. It should also teach your reader something about you that will help them connect with you and your book.[86] Importantly, your preface should not be confused with a foreword. A foreword is

---

[82] "Outlining a Nonfiction Book: 3 Steps to Success." *Reedsy*, https://blog.reedsy.com/guide/nonfiction/how-to-outline-a-nonfiction-book/ Accessed 27 May. 2023.

[83] Jalkiewicz, Liz. "Disclaimers for Books: What You Need to Know." *The Dietitian Editor*, 6 May. 2023, https://thedietitianeditor.com/disclaimers-for-books/ Accessed 27 May. 2023.

[84] MasterClass, "What's the Difference? Preface, Prologue, Introduction, and Foreword" MasterClass, August 23, 2021, https://www.masterclass.com/articles/preface-prologue-introduction-difference#48iObdR9eatXZIOt0Fi2qW Accessed 27 May. 2023.

[85] MasterClass, "What Are the Different Parts of a Book?" MasterClass, September 8, 2021 https://www.masterclass.com/articles/what-are-the-different-parts-of-a-book#6ExzpaMfnrNP7VCEPzNE7Y Accessed 27 May. 2023.

[86] "What Is a Preface? Characteristics and Examples." *Reedsy*, https://blog.reedsy.com/guide/parts-of-a-book/preface/ Accessed 27 May. 2023.

an introductory section written by someone other than you, who can help lend credibility to your book.[87] They are mostly written by prominent persons who can help increase the profile of your book and attract casual readers who may decide to purchase your book based on the endorsement of the foreword's author.[88] If you know such a person, and are interested in having them prepare a foreword to your book, feel free to engage them if their support would be helpful. If not, the preface is the appropriate way to begin your book.

- Chapters-In many cases, writers know the general concept of what they want to write about, but still somehow experience difficulty when starting. In your case, you can consider starting your chapters with a story, a question or a thesis statement.[89] Whatever you decide, your chapter needs an introduction that grabs your readers' attention. In addition to this, it needs an expression of the central point of the chapter. This could be a sentence or a few sentences. With this, you can begin to develop the central idea throughout the chapter,

---

[87] MasterClass, "What's the Difference? Preface, Prologue, Introduction, and Foreword" MasterClass, August 23, 2021, https://www.masterclass.com/articles/preface-prologue-introduction-difference#48iObdR9eatXZIOt0Fi2qW Accessed 27 May. 2023.

[88] MasterClass, "What's the Difference? Preface, Prologue, Introduction, and Foreword" MasterClass, August 23, 2021, https://www.masterclass.com/articles/preface-prologue-introduction-difference#48iObdR9eatXZIOt0Fi2qW Accessed 27 May. 2023.

[89] "How to Write a Book Chapter in 7 Simple Steps for Your Nonfiction Book." *SelfPublishing.com : The #1 Resource for Self-Publishing a Book*, 22 Aug. 2019, https://selfpublishing.com/how-to-write-a-book-chapter/ Accessed 27 May. 2023.

paragraph by paragraph. When that's done, you can conclude your chapter, perhaps with a recap or summary of the chapter, and then write a few sentences transitioning to your next chapter. At a basic level, this is how each of your chapters should be developed.[90] The precise style or technique is left to your creativity. Additionally, how you structure your chapter is left to your determination. You may write it as one continuous prose, you may introduce sub-headings, or you may utilise lists. Whatever you decide, try your best to achieve uniformity of structure across all your chapters. Similarly, endeavor to write chapters that are as equally weighted in terms of length as possible. Lastly, consider the titles of your chapter. If the title you chose when creating your book outline still aptly describes the contents of your chapter, you may stick to it. If not, you need to select an appropriate chapter title which may take the form of a sentence fragment, a prepositional phrase, a full sentence, a descriptive phrase, a headline, or simply a number.[91]

---

[90] "How to Write a Book Chapter in 7 Simple Steps for Your Nonfiction Book." *SelfPublishing.com : The #1 Resource for Self-Publishing a Book*, 22 Aug. 2019, https://selfpublishing.com/how-to-write-a-book-chapter/ Accessed 27 May. 2023.

[91] "How to Write a Book Chapter in 7 Simple Steps for Your Nonfiction Book." *SelfPublishing.com : The #1 Resource for Self-Publishing a Book*, 22 Aug. 2019, https://selfpublishing.com/how-to-write-a-book-chapter/ Accessed 27 May. 2023.

- Postface- A postface is a brief article or note placed at the end of your book.[92] Unlike the preface, this can be written by you or another person. It serves to support what was said throughout the book and to proffer a conclusion on the subjects discussed in the book.[93]

- About the Author- This is the part of the book where you tell the reader who you are, why you wrote your book, what else you've written or done, and if you have a platform, how your readers might be able to reach you.[94] Essentially, this is where you include all the details you considered at the pre-writing stage when thinking about who you are in relation to your book.

- Blurb- This is the back cover of your book which outlines a short statement of about 100 to 200 words explaining to your reader why they need to buy your book. It should be simple, attention-grabbing, focused on the problem that your book addresses and indicative of how your book provides solutions to that problem.[95] In doing this, your blurb may incorporate rhetorical questions,

---

[92] "Definition of POSTFACE." *Postface Definition & Meaning - Merriam-Webster*, https://www.merriam-webster.com/dictionary/postface Accessed 27 May. 2023.

[93] "Definition of POSTFACE." *Postface Definition & Meaning - Merriam-Webster*, https://www.merriam-webster.com/dictionary/postface Accessed 27 May. 2023.

[94] "About the Author: 7 Examples to Help You Write Yours - Self Publishing School." *Self Publishing School*, 23 May 2022, https://self-publishingschool.com/about-the-author/ Accessed 27 May. 2023.

[95] Christian McClean, "How To Write a Nonfiction Book that Sells: A Comprehensive Guide" *CEM Writing Services*, https://www.cemwritingservices.com/blog/2020/12/20/the-ultimate-nonfiction-book-guide Accessed 27 May. 2023.

outline alarming statistics, or reveal a truth about you that your potential readers might connect with. Overall, the objective is to prove why your book matters to your potential reader.

There's no pressure to approach your outline in any particular order. You can write the chapter that's easiest to start even if it's your last chapter. You may even begin by writing your blurb. Whatever feels right, simple and natural for you to do, do that. You can always go back to make sure that everything mends together seamlessly. The goal, for now, is just getting words on to the page.

Do not be afraid if your work isn't as good as you want it to be because it isn't supposed to be. Your draft is the raw version of what will be your finished work, once refined. All you need to do is focus on writing, and as long as you're writing, you're progressing.

If at any time, you feel stuck, consider whether you have enough information to continue writing. It's possible to feel as though you have tons to say about a subject, before drafting, only to find out that you don't. Concepts, ideas and experiences oftentimes appear more voluminous in our heads than they actually are when written. The solution for this is to read, read, read.

Writing is a derivative that comes from reading.[96] Reading will help you bolster your content,[97] and develop creative writing

---

[96] jerichowriters. "99 Quotes About Writing by the World's Greatest Writers | Jericho Writers." *Jericho Writers*, 17 Nov. 2020, https://jerichowriters.com/99-quotes-about-writing-by-the-worlds-greatest-writers/ Accessed 27 May. 2023.

strategies, word choices and syntax control which will all help to supplement your writing skills.[98]

Another key consideration when drafting is ensuring that you reference and cite your sources, where necessary. You never want to pass someone else's work off as your own. Not only is it unethical and dishonest, it also denies your readers the opportunity to find out more information by looking up the sources you used. So, as you write, cite your sources in accordance with a recognized citation style whether it be the Chicago citation style, the MLA (Modern Language Association) style, the APA (American Psychological Association) style, or otherwise.

## Revising

The revision stage is the refining stage of writing. It's the point where you focus on your language, formatting, and style of writing. It's also the point where you ensure that your book has accomplished its objective in a clear and organized manner.[99] For this reason, revision ought not to be rushed.

---

[97] "How Reading Will Help Your Writing and Add Pleasure to Your Life." *How Reading Will Help Your Writing and Add Pleasure to Your Life*, 12 Nov. 2021, https://www.routledge.com/blog/article/how-reading-will-help-your-writing-and-add-pleasure-to-your-life Accessed 27 May. 2023.

[98] MasterClass, "Become a Better Writer by Reading: 5 Ways Reading Improves Writing", December 1, 2021, https://www.masterclass.com/articles/become-a-better-writer-by-reading Accessed 27 May. 2023.

[99] "Revising Drafts; the Writing Center • University of North Carolina at Chapel Hill."https://writingcenter.unc.edu/tips-and-tools/revising-drafts/#:~:text=Revision%20literally%20means%20to%20%E2%80%9Csee

To revise, you literally have to view your work with a fresh and critical perspective. That's why, it's advisable to wait a few hours or days before doing it. Taking some time away from your book can help you acquire a healthy detachment from what you wrote and increase your chances of being objective when considering the changes to be made.[100] In so doing, you may see the need to restructure sentences, rewrite sections, shift the order of ideas, change the focus of some parts, and even delete sections that are not useful for the purpose of supporting the main idea.[101]

It's also useful to read out loud in order to amplify the problems and errors to be addressed.[102] To assist with this process, here are a few questions you should answer.

1. Does the book have a clear and concise main idea? Is this idea made clear to the reader early in the book, preferably in your preface?

---

,your%20presentation%2C%20reviving%20stale%20prose. Accessed May 27, 2023

[100] Revision Checklist for Paragraphs and Essays." *ThoughtCo*, 3 July 2019, https://www.thoughtco.com/an-essay-revision-checklist-1690528 Accessed May 27, 2023

[101] "Revising Drafts; the Writing Center • University of North Carolina at Chapel Hill." https://writingcenter.unc.edu/tips-and-tools/revising-drafts/#:~:text=Revision%20literally%20means%20to%20%E2%80%9Csee,your%20presentation%2C%20reviving%20stale%20prose. AccessedMay 27, 2023

[102] "Revision Checklist for Paragraphs and Essays." *ThoughtCo*, 3 July 2019, https://www.thoughtco.com/an-essay-revision-checklist-1690528 Accessed May 27, 2023

2. Does the book have a specific purpose (such as to inform, entertain, evaluate, or persuade)? Have you made this purpose clear to the reader?

3. Does the preface create interest in the topic and make your audience want to read on?

4. Is the structure of your book clear? Does each chapter develop logically from the previous one?

5. Is each chapter clearly related to the main idea of the book? Is there enough information in the book to support the main idea?

6. Is the main point of each chapter clear?

7. Are there clear transitions from one chapter to the next?

8. Are the sentences clear and direct? Can they be understood on the first reading? Are the sentences varied in length and structure? Could any sentences be improved by combining or restructuring them? The goal is to let your reader feel as though they cannot afford to omit any line of your writing because you have already omitted every word that they can spare.[103]

9. Are the words in the book clear and precise? Does the book maintain a consistent tone and style?

10. Does the book have an effective conclusion—one that emphasizes the main idea and provides a sense of completeness?

---

[103] A quote by **Ralph Waldo Emerson.** jerichowriters. "99 Quotes About Writing by the World's Greatest Writers | Jericho Writers." *Jericho Writers*, 17 Nov. 2020, https://jerichowriters.com/99-quotes-about-writing-by-the-worlds-greatest-writers/ Accessed May 27, 2023

# Editing

The kind of editing done at this stage differs from the kind of editing we do while we write. While we write, we may change a few words in a sentence, revert to a previous paragraph, change a semi-colon to a colon, or write a few more sentences where a smoother transition is needed. This is known as ongoing editing.[104]

What we do at the end of the drafting stage is the draft edit.[105] This is where we focus on entire finished work to ensure that it is clear, concise, and grammatically correct. This means that at this stage, you'll need to pay attention to punctuation, spelling and capitalization and word usage.

The main difference between what we do at this stage and what we did at the revision stage is that at the revision stage our goal was to evaluate the overall structure of the book to make sure that it effectively communicated our intended message. At this stage however, the focus is on the technical aspects of the writing, such as punctuation, spelling, capitalization, and word usage.

Here are ten key questions to ask when editing.

1. Are all of the sentences clear and complete?
2. Can short sentences be improved by combining them?

---

[104] "How Do You Edit an Essay?" *ThoughtCo*, 2 Nov. 2019, https://www.thoughtco.com/what-is-editing-1690631 Accessed May27, 2023

[105] "How Do You Edit an Essay?" *ThoughtCo*, 2 Nov. 2019, https://www.thoughtco.com/what-is-editing-1690631 Accessed May27, 2023

3. Can any long sentences be improved by separating them into smaller units and then recombining them?
4. Can any verbose sentences be made more succinct?
5. Do the verbs and subjects agree?
6. Are all verb forms correct and consistent?
7. Do pronouns refer clearly to their respective nouns?
8. Do all modifying words and phrases refer clearly to the words they should be modifying?
9. Are the words correctly spelt?
10. Are the sentences properly punctuated?

Evidently, editing is going to take you some time, but that time is worth investing in order to produce a high-quality book. Also, once you're done self-editing, you should hire a copyeditor to help you capture the mistakes you might have overlooked. They can also help you rephrase or reorganize content to improve clarity and readability, and make sure that any citations and references you may have used are accurate and properly formatted.

Although copyediting can add to the cost of producing yourbook, it's a worthy investment given how distracting typographical errors and chunky sentences can be to your readers. Additionally, mistakes tend to lower your credibility, making it hard for your audience to receive your message.

Your best chance at producing an error-free and polished book is by having it reviewed and corrected by an objective editor which you can find online on Fiverr. According to your budget, you can choose the range that you're willing to pay, and select the appropriate editor with adequate experience to review your work.

## Proofreading

The proofreading stage of writing is the final step in the editing process. This is where you review your book for any remaining errors before it is published. It's also the point where you check for formatting issues and make sure that all citations and references are accurate and properly formatted.

Proofreading is yet another step you should consider outsourcing. Although you can carefully review your book yourself, your best chance of producing a book without mistakes is by having it proofread by someone else. Experienced and affordable proofreaders can also be found online on Fiverr.

# Part 3

# The Self-publishing Stage

> "The pain of an unpublished manuscript is akin to the trauma of bearing an unborn".[106]

For some, publishing is the easy part. The content is complete and all that's left to do is to share it with the world. For others, publishing is where it gets hard. This is where we have to be open and vulnerable and share a piece of ourselves with others. Whether our book is about us or not, when we publish it, in some form or fashion, we lay ourselves bare before the world. This, for most persons, is scary.

Knowing that people can share opinions, leave reviews and make comments about what we have done, is what leaves the majority of writers, unpublished. It's far easier to keep our secret project, a secret, than it is to open ourselves up to criticism, whether constructive or malicious. Even so, there's no other way to be become an author than by publishing what we've written.

To distinguish ourselves from the millions who have gotten to this point, and let fear hold them back, we have to believe that

---

[106] A quote by poet and author, Anurag Shourie. "Publishing Books Quotes (27 Quotes)." https://www.goodreads.com/quotes/tag/publishing-books Accessed May 27, 2023

our best is good enough. In fact, beyond this, we have to believe that we are good enough to share our best with the world.

Whatever the reason for writing your book, this is the time to remember it! It is worth you pushing past fear to accomplish it! It is worth you taking the bold step to finally publish!

Thanks to self-publishing platforms, you no longer have to wait on traditional publishing companies! You can get your book directly to your readers by following the steps below.

## Book Designing and Formatting

According to renowned American author, Vince Flynn, "[t]here's a lot more to publishing a book than writing it and slapping a cover on it."[107] This is the absolute truth, and moreso when it comes to self-published books. One of the tell-tale signs that a book is self-published is poor book design, and worse, a poorly designed book cover.

Although self-publishing is now widely accepted as a legitimate option for publishing books, it is still bedeviled by a few common stigmas. Self-published books can easily be regarded as low quality, low content, unedited books that are unwanted by 'real' publishers. To avoid this stigma, in addition to dedicating time, efforts and resources to the writing process, one of the services you need to invest in, is book design.

---

[107] "Vince Flynn Quote: 'There's a Lot More to Publishing a Book Than Writing It and Slapping a Cover on It.'" https://quotefancy.com/quote/1189743/Vince-Flynn-There-s-a-lot-more-to-publishing-a-book-than-writing-it-and-slapping-a-cover Accessed May 27, 2023

## Interior book design

Interior book design relates to the font, formatting and overall layout of your book. It is important to ensure that the visual appearance of your book is appealing and in line with what readers in your genre would expect. To achieve this, aim to comply with the following suggestions.

- **Trim size**: The trim size of your book is its actual size after the excess material required in production has been removed or "trimmed off". In determining the appropriate trim size for your book, consider its genre and select the trim size that is most commonly used in that genre. It is likely that this is what your readers will be expecting of your book. The most common trim size for books is 6" x 9" (15.24 x 22.86 cm),[108] but other trim sizes available on the Amazon KDP interface include 7.5" x 9.25" (19.05 x 23.5 cm), 8" x 10" (20.32 x 25.4 cm) and 8.5" x 11" (21.59 x 27.94 cm).[109]

- **Fonts**: The font that you choose should be easy to read and of an appropriate size for your audience. Depending on your genre and the age group of your target audience, select a font that they likely find visually appealing.

---

[108]"Print Options." *Print Options*, https://kdp.amazon.com/en_US/help/topic/G201834180 Accessed May 27, 2023

[109]"Print Options." *Print Options*, https://kdp.amazon.com/en_US/help/topic/G201834180 Accessed May 27, 2023

Common fonts include Times New Roman, Garamond, Bookman and Book Antiqua.[110]

- **Text Alignment**: Alignment relates to how the text is set on the page as well as the amount of space between words. Be sure to select options that will help to achieve a balanced alignment of the words on the page.[111] For instance, you may choose to align your headings in the centre, but choose the justification option for the body of your text.

- **Text Hierarchy**: Establish a hierarchy of font sizes amongst your chapter titles, headings, sub-headings, body, and so forth. This helps to make your content more digestible and alert your readers to various components of the text.[112] For instance, larger, emboldened headings can help alert your readers to what the smaller text in the body is about.

- **Illustrations**: Be sure to ensure that you own or obtain the rights of any art, graphics or other illustrations you wish to use to avoid copyright infringements. You should also ensure that all images are of the highest quality. This ensures the best visual results when printed.

---

[110] Staff, IngramSpark. "9 Tips for Interior Book Design." *9 Tips for Interior Book Design*, 7 Nov. 2017, https://www.ingramspark.com/blog/9-tips-for-interior-book-design Accessed May 27, 2023

[111] "Topic 6 - Introduction to Book Design." *Topic 6 - Introduction to Book Design*, https://kdp.amazon.com/en_US/help/topic/G202187820 Accessed May 27, 2023

[112] "Topic 6 - Introduction to Book Design." *Topic 6 - Introduction to Book Design*, https://kdp.amazon.com/en_US/help/topic/G202187820 Accessed May 27, 2023

If you have no idea how to make sure your book aligns with these guidelines, consider outsourcing book formatting to an experienced interior book designer. In particular, you should choose a designer who formats books in your genre, and for the Amazon KDP interface. These designers can be found online on Fiverr. Once properly formatted, your book will be ready to upload on the Amazon KDP interface. If not, the interface will reject your upload, and you'll have to fix the issues highlighted before it can be submitted.

## Book cover design

Unless you're a professional book cover designer, you probably need help with designing the cover of your book. At all times, you should avoid publishing a book with an "amateurish" looking cover.

A book cover that looks like it was designed by a non-professional will raise questions as to the quality of its content, and the credibility of the author. To avoid this, if you're not skilled in this area, develop a concept of how you want your cover to look, hire an experienced book cover designer, and then have them prepare options for you to choose from.

You can find book cover designers online on Fiverr. For the best results, be sure to choose a designer that works with books in your genre.

## Amazon Kindle Direct Publishing

Once your book has been designed and formatted, it is ready to be published on the Amazon KDP interface.[113] The Amazon KDP interface is arguably the best and most widely- used self-publishing platforms of the many platforms available ( others include Ingramspark, Draft2Digital, Acutrack and Lulu).[114]

Through the Amazon KDP interface, you can publish your book in a variety of formats (paperbacks, ebooks and hardcovers) without paying any upfront costs or keeping any inventory. All you need to do is upload your book, and whenever someone orders it on Amazon, KDP will print it, deliver it, and subtract the printing costs from your royalties. In other words, Amazon KDP will print your book on demand, and make it available to customers worldwide.

To have your book published and ready for purchase in about 72 hours, follow these seven steps![115]

- Create a KDP account: Go to https://kdp.amazon.com . If you already have an Amazon account you can simply sign in as you would on Amazon. If you do not have an Amazon account, you will need to register with your

---

[113] "12 Options for Print on Demand Books (Options for Authors)." *Self Publishing School*, 12 May. 2022, https://self-publishingschool.com/print-on-demand-books/ Accessed May 27, 2023

[114] "12 Options for Print on Demand Books (Options for Authors)." *Self Publishing School*, 12 May. 2022, https://self-publishingschool.com/print-on-demand-books/ Accessed May 27, 2023

[115] "How Much Does It Cost to Self Publish a Book - Written Word Media." *Written Word Media*, 15 June 2022, https://www.writtenwordmedia.com/cost-to-self-publish/#:~:text=The%20estimated%20total%20cost%20to,others%20spend%20nothing%20at%20all. Accessed May 27, 2023

email address. Once that's done, click the "Create" button.

- Select the format of book you wish to publish: At this stage, you'll be asked to select either the eBook, paperback or series page option. Select the option you're interested in. If you're interested in creating a digital book. Select the eBook option. If you're interested in having copies printed and shipped to your customers, select the paperback option. Here, we'll focus on the paperback option. Once you can do this, you'll be able to do the same when publishing in other formats.

- Insert your book details: At this point, you'll be prompted to insert key details about your book. You'll get to select the language of your book, its title and subtitle, a description for your book, the name of the author(s), key words to help your customers find your book easily, which category or genre your book is in, and so forth. Carefully insert the details, and be mindful of the fact that this information is what will help drive traffic to your book. As such, your description should be captivating, your keywords should be accurate and your categories should be appropriate. You should also consider whether you'd like to publish using your real name or not.

- Upload your cover and manuscript: This part should be fast and easy once your cover and manuscript were formatted by someone who is experienced in preparing files for the Amazon KDP interface. All you have to do is select the files from your computer and click "Upload". Amazon KDP should accept them without hesitation. If however, the cover file and the manuscript file were not properly formatted, the interface will prompt you to make the necessary corrections before accepting them for publication. This is why it is a great idea to outsource formatting to someone from Fiverr.

- Get a free ISBN: An ISBN is an International Standard Book Number. It's what uniquely identifies your book internationally.[116] You will need one to be generated for your book before you can proceed. Fortunately, the Amazon KDP interface can assign one to you for free.

- Price your book: Insert the price for your book. At this point, the interface will let you know how much royalties you'll earn per purchase as well as how much will be deducted from your royalties for printing.

- Publish your book: Select "Publish" and wait for about 72 hours for your book to go live on Amazon.[117]

---

[116] "LibGuides: ISBN and ISSN Systems: General Information and Resources." *General Information and Resources - ISBN and ISSN Systems - LibGuides at American Library Association*, 28 June 2022, https://libguides.ala.org/isbn-issn#:~:text=The%20International%20Standard%20Book%20Number,book%2Dlike%20products%20published%20internationally. Accessed May 27, 2023

[117] "How Much Does It Cost to Self Publish a Book - Written Word Media." *Written Word Media*, 15 June 2022, https://www.writtenwordmedia.com/cost-to-self-publish/#:~:text=The%20estimated%20total%20cost%20to,others%20spend%20nothing%20at%20all. Accessed May 27, 2023

## Proof and authors' copies

Before you publish copies of your book for sale, you can consider publishing proof copies and/or author copies. A proof copy is a test copy of the book. It's solely for your review prior to publication on Amazon.[118] It features a "Not for Resale" watermark and does not have a bar code or an International Standard Book Number (ISBN) to identify it. It's meant for you to ensure that the book meets your expectations in terms of layout, cover design, colours, thickness, and so forth.[119] It also gives you the opportunity to experience the book as your readers would, and adjust it according to your likeness before publication.

On the other hand, an authors' copy is not an unpublished draft. Instead, it is a live and true copy your book. What distinguishes it from copies being sold to your readers is that it's available to you, only, at the cost of printing.[120] This affords you the opportunity to sell it in-person at whatever cost you choose,

---

[118] "Proof and Author Copies." *Proof and Author Copies*, https://kdp.amazon.com/en_US/help/topic/G7BBN68RYX5UMDZF#:~:text=Proof%20copies%20feature%20a%20%E2%80%9CNot,to%20you%20at%20print%20cost. Accessed May 27, 2023

[119] H, Paul. "Before You Publish: Get a Proof Copy." *Lulu Blog*, 7 July 2022, https://blog.lulu.com/what-is-a-proof-copy/#:~:text=This%20proof%20copy%20is%20your,before%20you%20sell%20your%20book. Accessed May 27, 2023

[120] "Proof and Author Copies." *Proof and Author Copies*, https://kdp.amazon.com/en_US/help/topic/G7BBN68RYX5UMDZF#:~:text=Proof%20copies%20feature%20a%20%E2%80%9CNot,to%20you%20at%20print%20cost. Accessed May 27, 2023

distribute it at book signing events, or share it with friends and family.[121]

It's entirely up to you whether you order proof or authors' copies. However, it's always advisable to order a few proof copies for review and to have a few authors' copies to share or sell directly. These can be ordered via the same Amazon KDP interface used to publish books.

---

[121] Lisa Shea, "Amazon Paperback Proof Copy vs Author Copy" https://lisashea.com/lisabase/writing/gettingyourbookpublished/createspace/amazon-proofcopy.html Accessed May 27, 2023

# Part 4

# The Marketing and Selling Stage

*"Writing a book without promoting it is like waving to someone in a dark room. You know what have you done but nobody else does."*[122]

High-quality books don't sell themselves. Even if you write the most wonderful book in the world, people won't buy it if they don't know it exists. The success of your book ultimately depends on how effectively you market and promote it.

Whether offline or online, you need to do your best to get your book in front of readers. This takes time, money, effort and bravery. Even if you're low on these resources, you need to be willing to use whatever you have to the best of your ability.

You don't have to be perfect, and you don't have to know it all. You just have to do your best to get what you want: your book to make an impact! Here are a few tips on how you can do this.

## Offline strategies

Let's start offline. Many people think that anything that's offline is too old-fashioned to be effective. That's not true! Offline

---

[122] A quote by freelance publicist, Madi Preda. Book Marketing Quotes (28 Quotes)." *Book Marketing Quotes (28 Quotes)*, https://www.goodreads.com/quotes/tag/book-marketing Accessed May 27, 2023

marketing strategies allow you to interact more directly with your audience. This way, they get to connect with, and see the benefit of learning about you and your content. These connections can be established through:

- radio and television interviews about your book;
- one-on-one conversations with persons;
- newspaper articles about your book;
- a book launch event;
- book clubs; and so forth.

Of course, the strategy you choose should be informed by what you're comfortable with, can afford and have access to. Whatever you choose, be intentional about ensuring that your choice isn't being determined by fear. For instance, don't let fear be the reason why you opt to do a newspaper article instead of an interview, or host a book club instead of a book launch. Do your best to overcome fear and use every available opportunity to promote your book! An added benefit of this might be finally doing that thing that you always wanted to do, but never had the courage to try!

## Online strategies

The internet has revolutionized the way we do everything, and this includes book promotion. With a wide range of tools and techniques, the possibilities are endless, and more than likely, you already have the skills you need to promote your book online. If not, you likely know persons whom you can ask for help.

With some time, effort, and if you can afford it, some money as well, here are some strategies you can implement to market your book online.

- Utilise social media platforms to promote your book, and ask your friends and family to do the same.
- Hire a social media influencer to promote your book on their platform. This way, you can reach a larger audience and generate more sales. This however, will add to your expenses and may even require you entering into an Influencer Agreement with the influencer. It's none-the less worth it because this is a great way to reach a demographic that you might not be able to market to yourself. If you choose this option, a great resource that can help you ensure that your partnerships with influencers run smoothly is the Write the Book Influencer Agreement Template. You can find it on https://writethebookgy.com/. Don't commit to any influencer arrangement blindly! Get the template and get the clarity you need!
- Create more content to support your book. For instance, write about topics related to your book on blog sites and writing platforms such as https://medium.com/ or https://ghost.org/ , and then refer your readers to your book.
- Encourage your readers to leave reviews on Amazon. Great reviews encourage potential readers to buy your book.
- Create a website around your book. This helps build community with your audience who can learn more

about you and your content before and after they purchase. This also makes it easier for you promote any other products or services you might have created around your book.

## Taxes

You should definitely contact the Revenue Authority in your jurisdiction to find out how you can achieve good standing with regard to your earnings from book publishing. Although your business may exist solely online, you might have tax obligations in the country or State you live in. The best place to get information on this is your Revenue Authority. They are best able to tell you:

- whether you need to obtain a Business Licence;
- whether you need to pay taxes;
- how much taxes you may need to pay;
- when your taxes become due, and so forth.

These are critical considerations for you to take into account as a successful self-published author. In the meantime, it's useful to keep a record of all the expenses you incur in relation to book-publishing. This is information your Revenue Authority may be interested in when informing you about your obligations, if any.

# Postface

Congratulations! You have made it through the Write the Book Handbook. More importantly, you have also either completed your own book, made significant strides in doing so, or at the very least, amassed the information needed to get your book to publication. This is a wonderful accomplishment, and you ought to be proud!

As Stephen King rightly said, "[b]ooks are a uniquely portable magic." With yours, you can change the world!

More than likely, your first book will not be your last. There may be many more books, businesses and ideas inside of you. Don't limit yourself. Keep going. Bring them to life. Keep writing. Keep publishing, and always remember,

'your best is good enough, and done is better than perfect'.

# The Author

I am a simple gal with a simple goal: ***getting the books inside of aspiring authors into the hands and hearts of their readers***! I do this through this book and the other resources available on, https://writethebookgy.com/.

Beyond this, I am a Guyanese educator, entrepreneur, and Attorney-at-law. If you want to read more of my work, you can get a copy of my other book called, ***Grieving while Christian***. In it, I give a brief account of my thought process while navigating grief as a devout Christian. Essentially, I share the thoughts that have helped me reconcile my belief in a good God with the devastating loss of my beloved father.

It was certainly a pleasure writing to you! If this book has been helpful, please tell a neighbor, tell a friend and of course, leave a review on whichever platform you bought it. I'd be happy to hear from you.

Made in the USA
Columbia, SC
17 June 2023